D0842702

If God Used Sticky Notes

For Those Who Need a Little Wisdom

From: God
To: All

Keep these
in your heart!
love,
God

Illustrations and text by

Chris Shea

HARVEST HOUSE PUBLISHERS

EUGENE, OREGON

Scripture quotations are taken from the King James Version of the Bible

Design and production by Garborg Design Works, Savage, Minnesota

If God Used Sticky Notes
for Those Who Need a Little Wisdom

Published by Harvest House Publishers
Eugene, OR 97402
www.harvesthousepublishers.com

ISBN-13: 978-0-7369-2155-8
ISBN-10: 0-7369-2155-9

Printed in China

08 09 10 11 12 13 14 15 16 / LP / 10 9 8 7 6 5 4 3 2 1

For Frank,
With gratitude for his uplifting thought.

Where do you think
God would put them, and what
do you think they would say

If God set out
a few sticky notes
to share his wisdom;
advice for you
to use today?

Maybe on the alarm clock
right beside your bed

Wake up!!
Rise and shine!
love,
God

When I am awake,
I am still with thee.

Psalm 139:18

or on your endless list
of things to do

To Do:

1. Bills ✓
2. School ✓
3. Wash ✓
4. Soccer
5. Grocery Store
6.
7. Carpool
8. Gym
9. Garden
10. Dentist
11.
12.
13.

5⁰⁰ OFF

Relax! I'll be nearby all day!

xo,

God

Take my yoke upon you, and learn of me; for I am meek and lowly in heart: and ye shall find rest unto your souls.

Matthew 11:29

on the basket of laundry
that's waiting to be folded

Aren't you so very blessed to have clean clothes and fresh sheets and towels? love, God

Whatsoever thy hand findeth to do, do it with thy might.
Ecclesiastes 9:10

the little address and
phone book on the desk

Anyone need the
blessing of your
voice today? (Hint!)
love,
God

Pleasant words are as a
honeycomb, sweet to the
soul, and health to the
bones.
Proverbs 16:24

the lunch you pack for work

16

Maybe you can
share a crust with
one of my birds
to day?
XO,
God

The time of the
singing of birds
is come.

Song of Solomon 2:12

the shoes you wear

or the side of your
bright red toolbox.

Your house looks especially lovely these days!

love,

God

Through wisdom is a house builded; and by understanding it is established.

Proverbs 24:3

What if they
surprised us all day long,
sweet small squares of paper
stuck on the things we touch

23

reminding us of God's ideas,
his wisdom, and his care.

A pink one on the car keys
we grab as we begin
the morning commute

a blue one on an apple
at the neighborhood
farmers' market

a yellow one
on a jacket
with a ten-dollar bill
tucked into a pocket

or a lavender one
on the bedroom windowpane,
the last sight
we see at night.

Of course, if we really think about it,

God's sticky notes are all around.

Heavenly advice
always finds a way

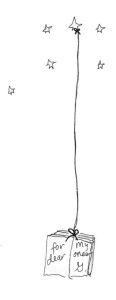

37

in bushels full of
fresh reminders
every single day

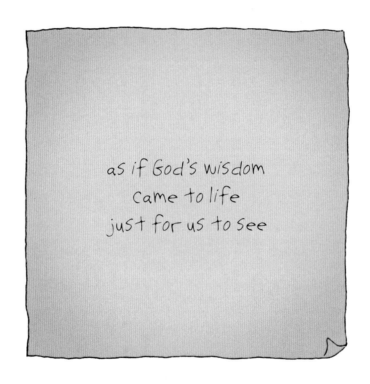

as if God's wisdom
came to life
just for us to see

in all the ordinary pathways
life beckons us to follow...

TODAY'S PATH

AM ☆ Tennis ☐
     ★ Lunch ☐
     ☆ Dentist ☐

P.M. ☆ LAUNDRY ☐
     ☆ COMMITTEE Meeting ☐
     ★ Walk dog ☐
     ★ Grocery store ☐
     ★ Bake pie ☐

a phone call
from a trusted friend
that seems from
out of the blue

45

a book we open up at random
to words we need to see

No matter how
scared you
may be,
please
remember
God is

always near!
He loves you!

He made you!

the sight of courageous
little green sprouts
coming up through the snow

or the guiding presence
of a familiar star
showing us where we are.

Each one a
kind of sticky thought,
written not by pen and ink

52

steadfastness

warmth

comfort

innocence

softness

faithfulness

but written nonetheless
for every heart upon the earth
to hold on to forever.

Where would I
like to see one,
and what would I
like it to say

if God put a
little sticky note
that shared his wisdom
just for you today?

I'd like him
to put it afloat
on a safe little boat
made of wood

and I'd like it to say,
as only God could

Let my wisdom and advice guide you through life's stormiest seas.
XO, God

(over →)

P.S. Remember This:

His candle shined
upon my head,
and ... by his light
I walked through
darkness.
Job 29:3